THIS BOOK BELONGS TO:

_____

WELCOME TO ARKANSAS

Dedicated to all the explorers.

ISBN 978-1-958985-80-9

www.joeysavestheday.com

A Mimi Book

Arkansas gets its name from the Quapaw people, a Native American tribe who lived along the Arkansas River. Early French explorers heard the Algonquian word for the Quapaws, which meant "people who live downstream," and wrote it down as Arkansas. The state later adopted this spelling, but in 1881 lawmakers decided the official pronunciation should be "Arkansaw."

Arkansas was the twenty-fifth state to join the Union. It officially joined on June 15, 1836.

25th

Arkansas is located in the Southern region of the United States and is bordered by six states: Missouri, Tennessee, Mississippi, Louisiana, Texas, and Oklahoma.

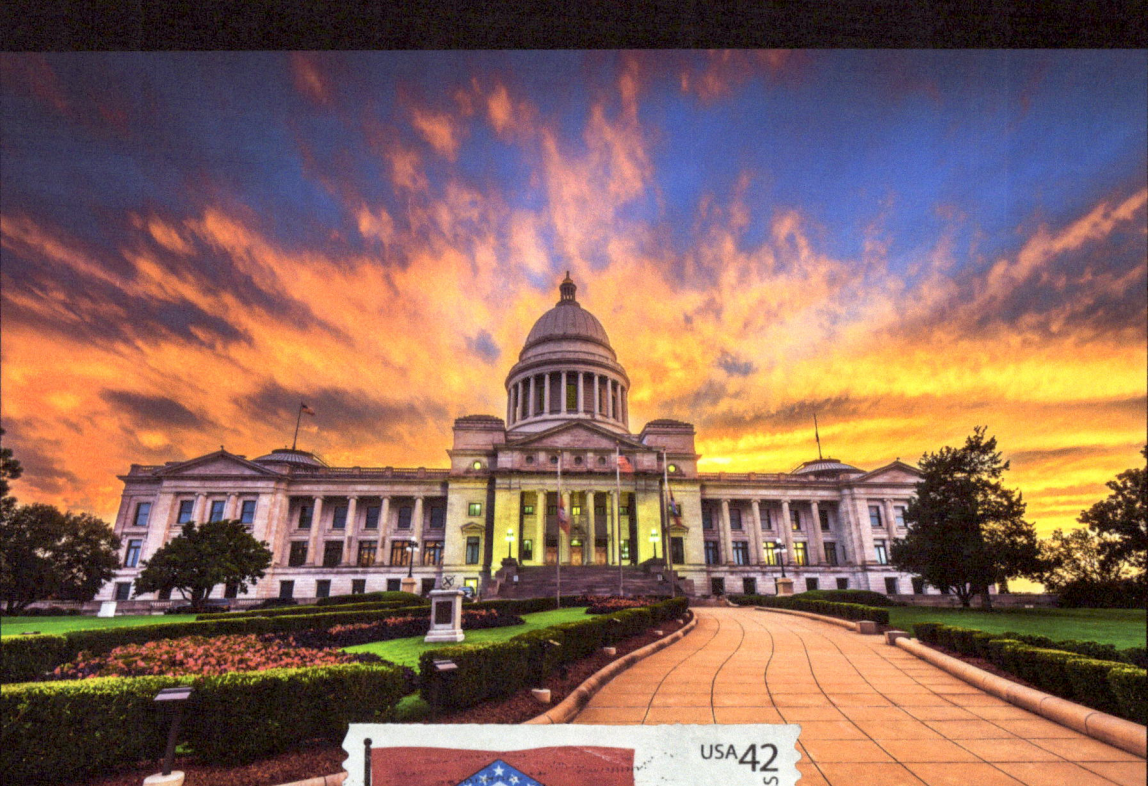

Little Rock, Arkansas, has an estimated population of about 204,770 people.

Arkansas

Arkansas is the twenty-ninth largest state in the United States by area.

Arkansas

Northern Arkansas

There are approximately 3,090,000 people residing in the state of Arkansas.

Hot Springs, Arkansas

Scott Joplin (1868–1917) was born in Texarkana, Arkansas, and became known as the "King of Ragtime." A gifted pianist and composer, he transformed American music with lively, syncopated rhythms that blended African American traditions with classical influences. His most famous works, including Maple Leaf Rag and The Entertainer, shaped the sound of the early 20th century.

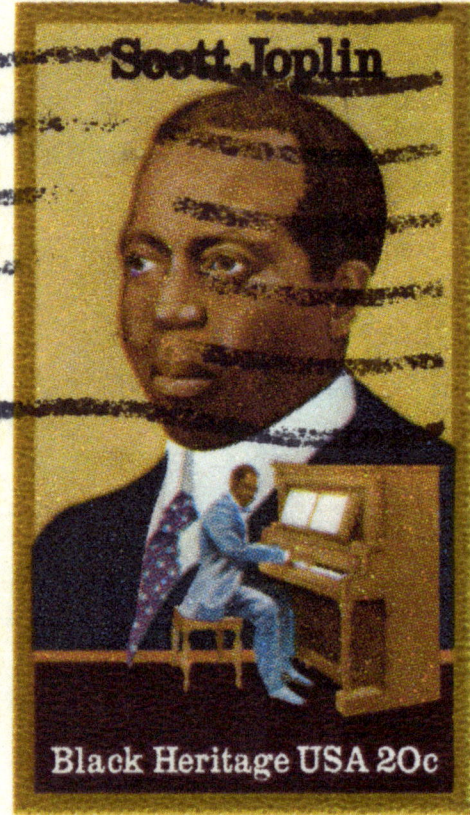

Scott Joplin

Black Heritage USA 20c

Arkansas is known for a delicious, creamy snack called cheese dip. It was first created in North Little Rock in 1935 and has become one of the state's most beloved foods. Arkansas even hosts cheese-dip competitions where people taste different versions and vote for their favorites. It's a fun, flavorful part of the state's history, and many Arkansans grow up enjoying it at family gatherings, football games, and local restaurants.

Arkansas

There are 75 counties in Arkansas.

Here is a list of twenty of those counties:

Ashley	Jefferson	Phillips	Searcy
Calhoun	Logan	Prairie	Sevier
Conway	Marion	Randolph	Sharp
Desha	Nevada	Saline	Union
Izard	Ouachita	Scott	Yell

Eden Falls is a beautiful waterfall tucked inside the Ozark Mountains along the Lost Valley Trail. The hike to the falls is short and full of surprises, like tall bluffs, a natural bridge, and a huge rock shelter called Cob Cave. In spring, the waterfall flows strong and sparkles as it drops into the canyon. Even in summer and fall, the trail stays cool and shady, making it a favorite spot for families exploring Arkansas.

Arkansas is the only state in the United States where anyone can dig for real diamonds and keep whatever they find. This happens at Crater of Diamonds State Park, a volcanic field turned public treasure hunt.

The Highway 23 Ozark Bridge crosses the wide Arkansas River in the town of Ozark. It connects travelers to the famous Pig Trail Scenic Byway, one of the prettiest drives in the state. The bridge is known for its tall steel truss design, which gives it a strong, geometric look as it stretches over the water. For many years, this crossing has been an important link between communities on both sides of the river.

BEAUTIFUL

Twin Falls is a beautiful double waterfall tucked inside the Ozark National Forest in northern Arkansas. Two narrow streams of water spill side-by-side over tall, rocky cliffs and land in a quiet pool below. The area feels peaceful and shaded, with mossy rocks, tall trees, and the sound of rushing water echoing through the forest.

The Arkansas state bird is the Northern Mockingbird. It was chosen as the state bird in 1929.

The official state flower of Arkansas is the Apple Blossom. It was chosen as the state flower in 1901.

OFFICIAL

THE Natural st🐻

~ AND ~

THE 🐻 ST8

Arkansas' state motto, "Regnat Populus," meaning "the people rule," was officially adopted in 1864.

THE

RULE

ARKANSAS
ARKANSAS
ARKANSAS
ARKANSAS

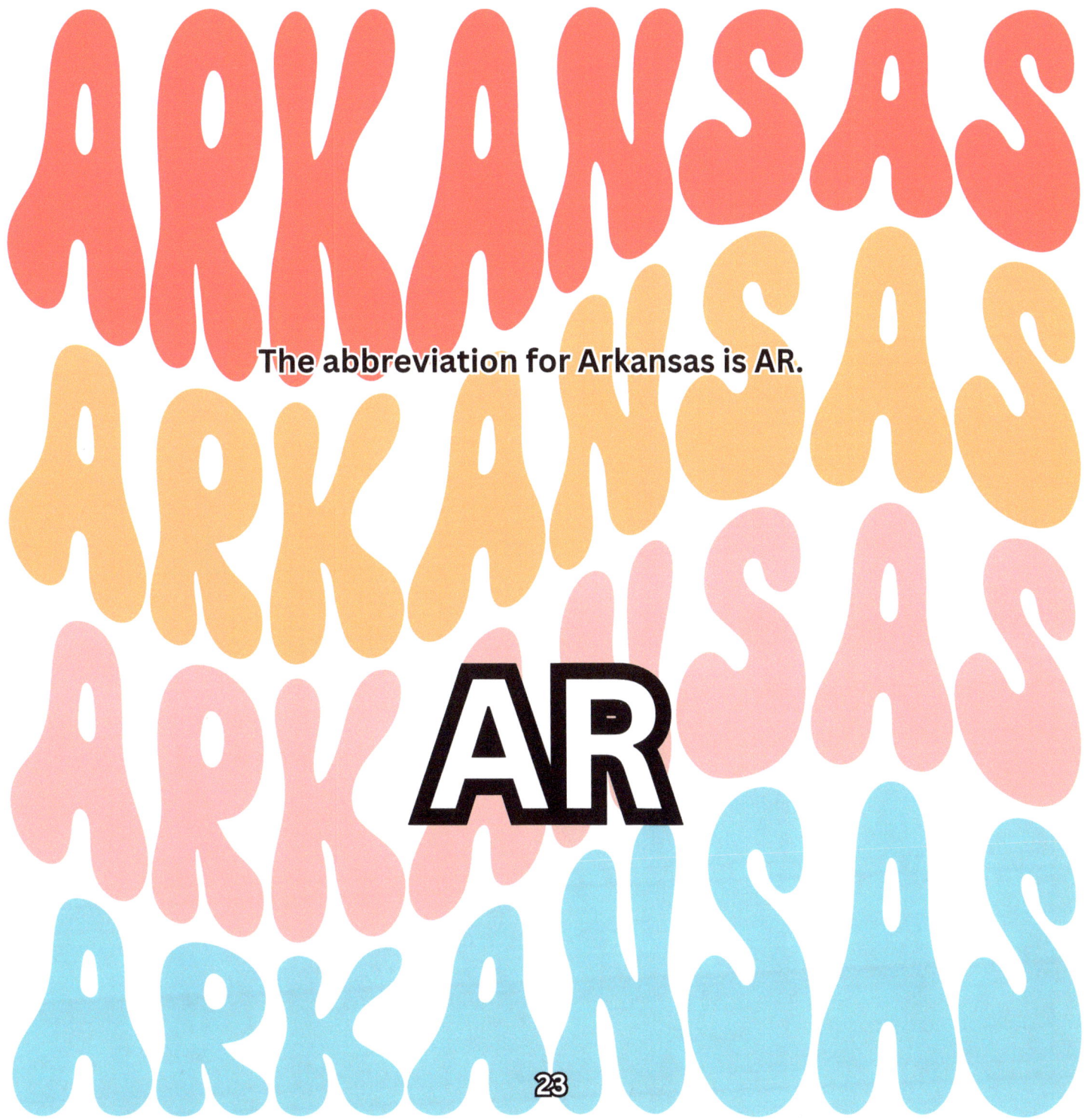

The abbreviation for Arkansas is AR.

AR

Arkansas' state flag was officially adopted in 1913.

Some crops grown in Arkansas are corn, cotton, soybeans, and wheat.

Some animals that live in Arkansas are black bears, bobcats, coyotes, foxes, and snowy owls.

Arkansas is characterized by considerable temperature variability throughout the year. The highest temperature recorded in the state was 120 degrees Fahrenheit, which occurred in the Ozarks on August 10, 1936. In contrast, the lowest temperature documented was -29 degrees Fahrenheit (29 degrees below zero), recorded in Pond, Arkansas, on February 13, 1905.

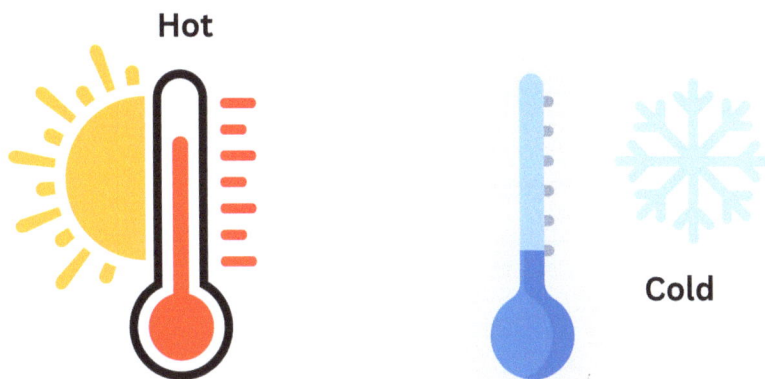

Hot

Cold

ZOO

The Little Rock Zoo is located in the heart of Little Rock, Arkansas, and is home to hundreds of animals from around the world. Kids can see lions, elephants, rhinos, penguins, and playful primates, along with colorful birds and reptiles.

28

Mammoth Spring is one of the largest natural springs in the United States, and it sends out a huge flow of bright, clear water every hour. The spring creates a calm, blue lake before the water moves over the old stone dam that once powered a mill and later a small power plant. Today, families can walk along the edge of the lake, see the historic dam and buildings, and watch the water rush into the Spring River.

The largest airport in Arkansas is the Bill and Hillary Clinton National Airport, located in Little Rock, right in the central part of the state. It sits at 1 Airport Road, Little Rock, Arkansas, and serves as the main travel hub for people flying in and out of Arkansas. This airport connects travelers to cities all across the country and is known for its easy layout and friendly atmosphere. It's also sometimes called Adams Field, a name that honors an early Little Rock mayor who helped develop aviation in the area.

The Arkansas Travelers are a Minor League Baseball team based in North Little Rock, right along the Arkansas River. They play their home games at Dickey-Stephens Park, a bright and cheerful ballpark with great views of the downtown skyline. The Travelers are the Double-A affiliate of the Seattle Mariners, which means many future major-league players spend time on this team as they grow their skills.

FOOTBALL

The Arkansas Razorbacks are the most famous football team in the state, and they play in Fayetteville, in the northwest corner of Arkansas. Their home field is Donald W. Reynolds Razorback Stadium, a loud and energetic place filled with fans wearing bright red. The Razorbacks are known for their unique cheer, the "Woo Pig Sooie" call, which echoes through the stadium on game days.

The pine tree is Arkansas's state tree. It stays green all year and grows tall and straight, making Arkansas's forests smell fresh and woodsy. Pines have long needles and sturdy cones, and they're an important part of the state's history because they helped build homes, furniture, and even whole towns.

ARKANSAS

The Alligator Gar is Arkansas's state fish. It's a huge, ancient-looking fish with a long snout full of tiny teeth and tough scales that feel like armor. Even though it looks a little scary, the alligator gar is gentle and spends most of its time cruising through slow rivers and lakes.

Can you name these?

I hope you enjoyed
learning about
Arkansas.

To explore fun facts about the other 49 states,
visit my website at www.joeysavestheday.com.
You'll also find a wide variety of homeschool
resources to support joyful learning at home.
If you enjoyed this book, I would be grateful if
you left a review. Your feedback truly helps.
Thank you for your support!

TIME
TO SAY
GOODBYE

Check out these other interesting books in the 50 States Fact Books Series!

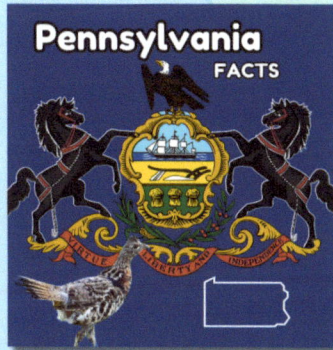

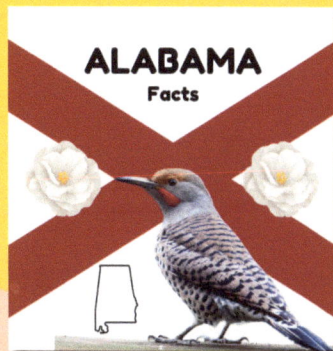

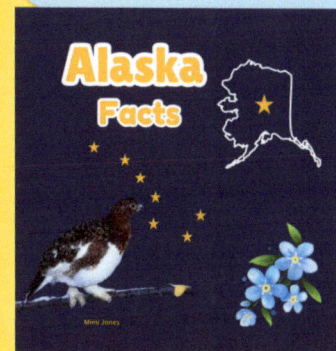

www.ingramcontent.com/pod-product-compliance
Lightning Source LLC
Chambersburg PA
CBHW041549040426

42447CB00002B/104